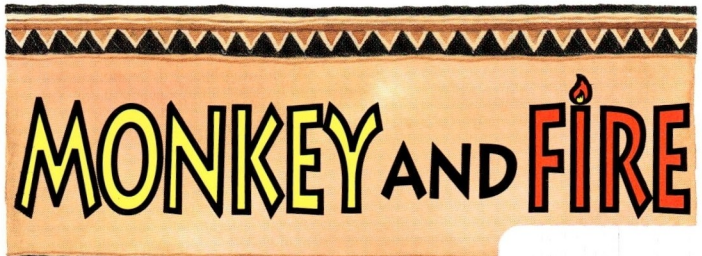

*A Story from Africa*

Monkey lived alone
in a little house
beside a river.

Sometimes Monkey felt lonely,
and one day he set out
to find a new friend.

Monkey walked and walked,
until at last
he saw something
bright and beautiful
dancing in the breeze.

Monkey walked closer.
"Who are you?"
he asked gently.

"I am Flower," it said.

"Will you come with me
and be my friend?"
asked Monkey.

"I grow in the soil,"
said Flower.
"I can't come with you
and be your friend."

So Monkey
went home alone.

When Monkey opened
his door the next day,
he saw a bright
and beautiful pattern
in the sky.

"Who are you?"
asked Monkey.

"I am Rainbow,"
said the pattern.

"Will you come with me
and be my friend?"
asked Monkey.

"I come and go
from the sky,"
said Rainbow.
"I can't come with you
and be your friend."

Rainbow slowly faded
from the sky.

And Monkey
closed his door.

Monkey searched
for a friend
all the next day.
But he found no-one.
Then he saw
a bright flickering light,
crackling in the grass.

Monkey thought it was
the most beautiful thing
he'd ever seen.

"Who are you?"
he asked.

"I am Fire," it said.

"Will you come with me
and be my friend?"
asked Monkey.

Fire moved closer to Monkey.
It made him feel warm.

"Yes, I will be your friend,"
said Fire.
"I will visit you tomorrow.
Lay a trail of sticks
and leaves so that I can
find my way."

The next morning
Monkey got up early.
He was very excited.

He laid a trail of sticks
and leaves to his door.
Then he sat down
and waited for his friend.

Suddenly, he heard a sound
like cracking whips
and hissing snakes.

He opened his door.
He saw Fire approaching,
red hot and roaring.

Monkey was very frightened.
He rushed to get his broom.
Then he swept the trail
of sticks and leaves away
from his door,
into the river.

Blazing Fire rushed past
Monkey, into the river.

It sizzled and steamed
in the water.
Then it disappeared
altogether.

Since that day, water has been used to put out fires.

And Monkey has been much more careful about looking for new friends.